THE P.L. LYFE

LYFE

FROM PRISON TO PEACE

BY

ANTHONY J. GONZALEZ

For my son, Dominic C. Taylor.

Life is what it is.

You must be ready for it.

TABLE OF CONTENTS

FOREWORD

What can I say?

When it comes to writing, I am a man of few words. I struggled with writing this foreword because I don't see myself as a writer, and that's just one of the many, many reasons I am so proud of my man, Anthony Jae Gonzalez. He wrote a book! He originally wrote this book for his first-born, Dominic, but it's also now for his second, Jaelin. I figured the least I could do was get a few words down to celebrate this moment.

At home and in the family, we call this guy Papi. Maybe it's because he's the wise one, the one who watches over us and schools us when the time is right. I'll say that no matter what we call him, he has risen to a place where he's a solid example of what a man and a father should be: dedicated, passionate and giving.

By blood, Papi is my nephew. He is the son of my oldest sibling; however, he's closer to me in age than any of my siblings. We have always been close, and I love him like a brother. He is a big part of the man that I am today; I looked up to him for his swag, his charisma, and because he stood up for himself – he didn't let anyone tell him what to do. I admired that. I also admired that he told me the real deal, even when it came to the little things. We grew up in the 90s, and he was the one who told me to listen to music other than rap; he told me there were other choices out there, like Baby Face and After 7. This is important because his telling me things like this was about more than just music. It was about changing your world view – it was about knowing there was more to life than just one thing, or what everybody else around you was doing. It was about knowing there was more than what was right in front of you, readily available. For a while, I was out in the streets with Papi, but because of him I turned my life around. I moved to Florida, got married and made some different choices in life. I'm thankful to him.

The book you're about to read comes from a man who has vision. Yes, he can be an asshole sometimes (and I say that affectionately while also "keeping it one hundred"), but his intentions are solid. Whenever I shared my ideas with him, he was always that one person who'd say, "Let's do this." He knew that we needed to make something for ourselves and of ourselves if we wanted to see any type of success in life. To me, that's what this book is really about and what it represents.

With The P.L.U.S.H. Lyfe, Anthony Jae Gonzalez wants you to make something of yourself. He wants you to get out there and not be a knucklehead doing stupid shit just because everyone else is, or because you think that's the only way to live. There are many ways, MANY ways, of getting by in life. He is living proof. And now this book is too.

With love and gratitude,
Wilfredo Otero

INTRODUCTION

A Manifestation of Divine Will and Trust

This book is written out of my own personal views on the steps toward true happiness. It also captures the life experiences I've had that coincide with each of those steps. There may be some topics or issues that some of you may find questionable or debatable. If that's the case then I'm satisfied, because if you're thinking about it that means you're taking the necessary steps toward happiness: you're on a journey to examine life and all that it offers. To experience the best journey toward happiness, you can't simply ride along and accept what comes your way. You must question and keep questioning until you find an answer that works for you.

I consider that questioning and how I go about it my personal process for mental evolution. I think evolution is a seeking of truth.

There was a period in my life where I was living in such a way that lies were disguised as truths – and vice versa. I got caught up in a whirlwind of chaos that cost me my freedom and damn near could have cost me my life. Thankfully, by the grace of God, the strength of my family and my own intelligence, really, I was able to keep a tight hold on my own truth.

That truth included what I knew to be right and wrong – no matter who was doing what around me ... and no matter if I was joining them or not.

During that hectic, harrowing, violent and even beautiful time in my life, I knew one thing: I wanted to be happy and, if I wanted to be happy, it was going to be up to me to find my way back to truth – fully, and not in a half-assed kind of way. So I came up with some steps to take toward happiness. At first, these steps were just a guideline for me: a road map of destinations to follow whenever I felt lost, disappointed, or confused with the way things were going. But then I started sharing them with the people around me.

Every time, every time, I talked to someone who was about to do something wrong, stupid or "gangsta", I gave them advice while using my theory, and it worked. My theory helped them get their mind right and make better choices for themselves. That theory is pretty simple. I discovered that if I kept my focus on five elements, I would be good. I'd never falter and end up in chaos again. Those five elements are Peace, Love, Unity, Success and Happiness, or P.L.U.S.H.

There were times when my theory didn't work, however, and that was when I was talking to a person who didn't really want to change. As a result, I think the main ingredient in my theory working for you is that you have to want to take these steps. For me, I've tried everything else (and I mean everything), and P.L.U.S.H. works for me. It helps me understand how people are easily misled to believe lies instead of truth. It reminds me how to react; instead of being angry and disappointed by people, I can now sympathize and forgive. It also keeps me on track toward the goals I am trying to achieve for myself and the well-being of my family. It helps me evolve.

This book is a result of my continued evolution. Telling others about P.L.U.S.H. is my calling and future. I've decided I must share my experience with everyone I can and pay it forward, because I've been given the gift of freedom and the time to do so.

If there are indeed steps towards peace, love unity, success and happiness on earth, then I believe I've found them. I put this book together with hopes of guiding all of us on this beautiful planet towards P.L.U.S.H., because, if there is one thing that I know, it's that true peace doesn't come from your homies, your boss, your bank account or your kids. It comes from within.

You have to know yourself, so that you can trust yourself, so that you can BE yourself. This is not an easy task.

Welcome to the P.L.U.S.H. Lyfe.

PROLOGUE

There are many lies in this world that people are led to believe are true. The lie is indoctrinated into the psyche and, after a long enough time, what we're led to believe is the truth can in fact *become* the truth.

They say "truth hurts", and I am a firm believer in that. Yet, if we were never lied to then maybe the truth wouldn't be so painful.

I think about the national news story about the thirteen Turpin children in Riverside, California. Their parents chained them to their beds and led them to believe that the world was small – that the world that existed inside their home was everything. This helped keep the children captive until one child had a change of mind. That child didn't want to believe the truth they'd been given. That child knew these so-called truths to be lies and found a way to call the authorities, which led to their freedom. I call what these children experienced "true lies".

True lies are things that have become a tradition or a habit yet are founded upon lies. For example, "being eighteen years of age means you're an adult". The truth is that in America eighteen is merely the legal age you're granted some rights and responsibilities: it's the age at which you can vote, the age at which you can be tried as an adult in court, the age at which you're legally allowed to consent in every state. The lie is that simply being eighteen years old doesn't mean a person is a (mature) adult. It just means that person has spent eighteen years on this earth. *That* is the truth.

We go through life believing these true lies. We use them as our benchmarks for success: if you own a business, you will automatically be successful and happy. If you do what your parents say, you will be a good child. If you follow the law, you will be rewarded with freedom.

But what happens when you start to question these truths? What happens when you realize that what you've been taught is basically a lie (or based upon one)? And better yet, what happens when that lie is taught to you, or upheld by someone you love, idolize, trust or respect? You know what I think happens? Change.

You start to separate the truth from the lies. There is a certain type of revelation that happens in your mind, and suddenly there is a clarity that you've never seen before. I've got to tell you that this revelation, in whatever form it takes, is a beautiful thing. However, I can also attest to the fact that getting to a point of clarity doesn't happen overnight, and it definitely doesn't happen without putting in some work. That work becomes incredibly hard, and it can be uncomfortable.

I have learned that being uncomfortable is a feeling that nobody enjoys, and that reason alone is why change is so difficult. *Or is it?* It could be that change isn't as hard as we would like to believe, especially when we realize most of the things we believe to be facts aren't anything more than someone else's opinions.

Change is freeing. Change is growth. Change is necessary, especially if you want to live a life other than the one you've been given. Especially if you want to be happy. Change is just the first step to happiness. To me, it's that empty plate you're handed by your auntie at Thanksgiving. What you put on that plate makes all the difference.

So, once you've decided you're ready for change, how do you get to happiness? What are the steps? I believe you must first believe that happiness is foreseeable and that you can fill your plate with happiness.

I began believing in happiness during a very pivotal time in my life when I didn't seem to have any control over it or what was going to happen next – and I'd lost that control because I'd been consumed by true lies. It was then that I started to break down the steps I needed to take toward happiness, and I did that by working backwards. I looked at what I'd done, what actions I'd taken to lead myself to my present situation, and then reverse engineered a formula for happiness. It looked like this:

> *With unconditional respect comes **P**eace.*
> *With unconditional love comes **L**oyalty.*
> *With unconditional strength comes **U**nity.*
> *With unconditional **S**uccess comes money.*
> *With unconditional power and freedom comes **H**appiness.*

This is what I call P.L.U.S.H.

To achieve this divine happiness, or to live a P.L.U.S.H. Lyfe, we must change our mindset to one that is open-minded and honest, and we must be willing to take the necessary steps and do the work. If we are open-minded, honest and willing, we may realize that our traditions and habits are based upon the interpretations of others. Those interpretations, even when they're popular, even when they're the law, are not always correct.

Now, we can't blame the people we love for teachings us the wrong things, because that blame would go so far back in time so as to be truly saddening. In fact, let's take a moment to look at what our ancestors were taught, because their thinking and traditions have been passed down to us. Just think of all the true lies our ancestors experienced. From being told they were worthless due to the color of their skin, to being made to believe their gender made them inferior, to being told that what was rightfully theirs now belonged to someone else. It's now up to us to correct those true lies instead of passing them on. It's up to us to recognize the truth and separate the lies, so that we, the people of today, can agree to pass on the truth. True lies hurt both us and our children. We've tried many ways over the decades and centuries to work around these true lies, but now it's time to stop lying. We've paid for the mistakes of others and, if we don't change our ways, our youth will continue to pay for ours.

We've got to believe that the truth will lead us to P.L.U.S.H., true equality and freedom.

So, the only thing left to do is to become willing to accept that our outlook on life – our ways and actions – may need to be reevaluated. We may need to unlearn some old ideas to make space for new ones. This will make change a lot more comfortable and satisfying.

Once I began to reevaluate my life with P.L.U.S.H. in mind, I started to see real change. I started to see things with a clarity I'd never known and hadn't really been taught. I wrote this book to try to help those find their way before it is too late, like it almost was for me.

01

WHEN MORALS AND VALUES AIN'T ENOUGH

I was born into a kingdom of kings – that is, in Kings County Hospital in Brooklyn, New York. I was raised by a family with strong morals and values. If something was considered wrong, it was wrong. If it was right, there was no arguing about how right it was. It just was.

My father was a provider, a militant man from Puerto Rico. He was a man of the times. That meant he toed the line of the men who'd come before him, and those men were the absolute heads of their households. They were the type of men who took no type of mouth or backtalk from anyone, and if somebody crossed the line, they got popped. This included their wives. And their kids. I learned real quick not to cross my dad, ever. So did my mom.

The two of them met one day while my mom was out walking the block. Something was going down, and she happened to be around the corner in another neighborhood: my dad's block. He saw her, yelled out to her, and I think that was it. They were together from the get-go.

My mom was a strong black woman. She was feisty. Beautiful. But she was different, too. She was curiously ... different. My mom didn't fit any kind of mold, and sometimes I wonder if that's why she got into drugs. Maybe she was looking for herself, maybe she was looking for a high. I don't know what she found, except crack and anything else she could get her hands on. And she wasn't alone. My dad joined her.

I grew up in New Lots, an East New York neighborhood in Brooklyn. Our neighborhood was united, but everybody had their own section. Whoever had the most family or family power held down the block. For us, that meant we held down our street. We were tightly knit, and even a little bit grimy – you couldn't get away with nothin' on our block. Family was always watching out, whether you wanted them to or not. If you messed up, you faced repercussions.

Neighborhoods are interesting. Ours was especially so. It had the ability to change people. Or, maybe more accurately stated, it had the ability to not let people change. It was full of these invisible truths. My parents got caught up in that and drugs got in the way. They started to believe that drugs were the only way.

Despite my father and mother's brief encounter with drug use and drug dealing, I managed to stay strong. I had to. During that time, my siblings became my responsibility. I was in charge of making sure they were fed, that they got to school and that they stayed safe and out of trouble. I was only eleven or twelve years old at the time, and our home life was unstable, to say the least. I'd wake up to prostitutes at the breakfast table with their legs spread, ready for work. 'Cause that's where the drugs and the action were. I started to drown. The streets knew what was going on in our three-bedroom flat off Cozine Avenue and Pine Street in East New York. But outside of that, nobody else knew what was going on, or at least nobody who could really help.

We were on welfare, like many of the families in our neighborhood. At the beginning of the month, we'd have eggs over-easy on white rice as our meal of the day, or for dinner we'd have those tiny pigs in a blanket you could get out of the freezer section. When that ran out at the end of the month, we were knocking on the neighbor's door for something to eat. And by "we", I mean me. I was the oldest, and it was up to me to keep shit together. What we were going through was nobody's business. Our life was ours, but I needed help and that's when I turned to my dad's mother (*mi abuela*) and his sister (*mi titi*). My *abuela* (grandmother) and *titi* (aunt) did their best to make sure my siblings and I stayed together and off of the streets. To me, they are two of the strongest Puerto Rican women I know. They saved us. They saved me.

I love my family, and in my eyes the women in my family are strong in all the ways the men were not. It was the women who held the house down and kept it going while the men were out in the streets doing whatever. (To me, if I'm keeping it real, dudes ain't shit alone. The men have their roles, of course, but the women are the bedrock.) As the foundation and support structure of our family, these women showed me that, no matter what, family is what's most important, and family comes first before self. They taught me the value and power of unity. And I think that power was based upon pride. You must have pride for who and where you come from, and you must honor that, always. I must admit that while we were not rich with money, we were rich with that pride and the principles that followed from it. They taught me that you can be weak and still be strong. You can love someone else and still love yourself, and you can come from the streets but not be of the streets. They really were the foundation for everything. That foundation of unity they provided for me was, and still is, priceless.

I have siblings upon siblings. There's a lot of us. Being the oldest, I love them all just the same. I do my best to reach out to each and every one of them whenever the opportunity arises. I strive to keep that unity going between us and keep us all connected. And I look up to each of them. I watched them grow up, and I admire them for not following in my footsteps. Out of all of them, I am the only one who was a victim of the streets and has a jail record. Like my parents, perhaps, I started to believe in truths that were based upon lies.

I learned that if I was loyal to someone in the streets my loyalty would return in the form of money. I believed that my destiny, my *survival*, was connected to the economic system that ruled the streets and its hierarchy. And I realized the truth about America's system of capitalism; it was designed to work against me, a marginalized black man in Brooklyn. It was fabricated from lies – lies that were centuries old and were annihilated by the truths of the street, which didn't give a damn about old white guys and Wall Street, though which were still all about the Benjamins.

I learned morals and values come with a price.

I lost my way.

Remember, I knew right from wrong. My *abuela* and *titi* instilled that in me. I knew the importance of honesty, respect, loyalty – things that we must hold dear among ourselves, family, friends and within our communities. I had *my* morals and values, yet I'm here to tell you that plenty of folks in the streets also have theirs. It's just that our definitions aren't the same. When those morals and values are attached to true lies, there's a problem.

I'll admit, I tried to hold on to what I believed to be true about honesty, respect and loyalty, but these noble qualities didn't make my life in the streets easy. Those values are hard to apply among people who believe in being honest after it's too late, or who earn respect by waving a gun, or who show their loyalty by hitting somebody in the face "for you" because that person has spoken out of their neck. That's a sad path to learning loyalty, and lots of times I couldn't get off that path. There was no way out sometimes. I did try. I did my best to not do the types of terrible things that other guys did, and sometimes I'd get the short end of the stick for it. I wouldn't get the loyalty that others got, and I'd be fighting for common respect. No wonder I was angry all the time. I'm not saying I didn't do wrong: clearly I did, or I wouldn't have gone to jail. But trying to do good in the midst of doing wrong didn't always work out for me.

Society makes it hard for the young and the poor to realize what's truly righteous and what's not. Morals and values have been compromised for a chance in the limelight and that "mighty" dollar. Society and poor leadership have put a price on everything that is priceless. That is: respect, loyalty, strength, success, love, unity, happiness, freedom and peace – and on honesty most of all, which brings forth each of the above.

As much of a role that drugs and violence played in my life, I tried hard not to promote any of it to my siblings. I was completely honest with them and schooled them on the harsh realities of being in the streets. I am proud to have been an influence on them doing and striving for better.

Luckily, they didn't follow me down this path, and I didn't rub off on them the wrong way. As I watched them grow into the unique individuals they became, I always made it my business not to influence them with negativity. Like *titi* and *abuela*, I reminded them of *our* morals and values to let them know those were enough.

02

CRACKING THE CODE
TO RESPECT

When I started this book in the summer of 2007, I was in the Albany County Jail awaiting trial for conspiracy to distribute five kilos of crack-cocaine.

Based upon the court proceedings up to that point, I knew I was potentially facing up to twenty years in prison. I was only thirty years old. Before I was locked up, I remember thinking that my time was limited: I knew if I made the wrong choice on the streets, I'd be dead. The difference was that somehow the choices I'd made on the streets had been mine. In jail, all my choice was taken away.

When faced with life behind bars, you learn a lot about who you are and who you want to be, rather than what you might become.

While at Albany, I spent a lot of time soul searching and thinking. I thought about what made me tick. I thought about how I made decisions and what it was that caused me to react in certain ways or hold strong opinions about certain things. I did a lot of thinking, a lot. And because I had so much time on my hands, that thinking turned into this book.

All I did while I was there was buy pens and pads of yellow paper – and I went through a lot of yellow pads! I wrote my thoughts down every chance I got. When it was time for me to leave, I mailed my grandmother, mother and aunt copies of what I'd written. All for safekeeping, until… And what exactly that "until" meant was a big question mark.

At my trial, I was offered twenty years for conspiracy to distribute. I was a part of a sting operation that included at least twenty-six other people. The sentence included a ten-year mandatory minimum, which was related to the amount of crack cocaine I was charged with carrying. Back then, we were under the Anti-Drug Abuse Act of 1986 and for every 100:1 crack-to-powder drug quantity ratio held, you got ten years out of the gate. This was during the Regan era and the war on drugs, which was really just about making crack a black thing and waging a war on black and brown folks. The Fair Sentencing Act of 2010 reduced the statutory penalty for a crack-cocaine offense to an 18:1 ratio. Due to this change and by the grace of God, I was let out in five years instead of twenty.

I was sentenced to Fort Dix Federal Correctional Institute, a low-security federal prison for men in Fort Dix, New Jersey. During my five years there, I'd often find my quiet moments of clarity while working the laundry room (which was the job to have; prison likes to pay you twenty-five cents a day for hard labor, either making things like license plates or sewing shit. Instead of rehabilitation being the focus, we are free labor for an economy that doesn't include us).

Between the washing and folding, I realized I had actually already been living my life in line with my P.L.U.S.H. theory – even in the streets. It was just that the environment was wrong for it to work for me at the time. In my heart and soul, I knew that if I practiced respect, I'd experience peace in return. I believed that showing love could result in loyalty. I knew that we experience strength by relying on others, by being unified rather than thinking we are some individual, almighty self. I knew that success could produce money, which leads to power and freedom, and that when we can achieve all of those things we reach a level of happiness. Like a scientist looking for a cure and trying to break down the genetic code of microbes, I would think about this minute after minute, hour after hour, and it just felt *so real*.

I'd repeat the words over and over again:

*With unconditional respect comes **P**eace.*
*With unconditional love comes **L**oyalty.*
*With unconditional strength comes **U**nity.*
*With unconditional **S**uccess comes money.*
*With unconditional power and freedom comes **H**appiness.*

I started thinking about what was buried within these words, and I always found myself starting at the beginning: unconditional respect.

Respect. What does that mean? How do we achieve it? I knew I had to dissect the meaning of it and so, at one point, I created an equation:

Respect + Loyalty = Strength + Money + Power & Freedom

I was obsessed with this. I became a mad scientist; I just needed to test my theory. I was high on the belief that we *could* be happy, that we could obtain a sense of freedom, if we started by focusing on respect.

Prison is an interesting place to start talking about respect. You have a lot of different men coming from a lot of different places and bringing value systems with them that are based on anything from their culture to the crew they run with. I knew they all had an association with the word, just like I did.

I conducted a test in the Albany County Jail. I let inmates of different races, beliefs, and ages who'd been charged with different crimes read what I had been writing. Funny as it may seem, everyone I let read it came back to me and shook my hand. The level of respect they had for me rose, and I tried to hold them to the theory that respect is the beginning of all things. From there on out, I talked to everyone with respect (whether they were initially respectful or not) and it came back to me each and every time.

I want to take this chapter to break down a few things for you, starting with respect, and then I'll end with a bit of a confession.

RESPECT:
To show honor or esteem for; to have consideration or regard for.

You would be surprised how much lacking a regard for respect will limit your achievements in life. Think about it. You can spot a person a mile away who doesn't respect themselves or others. You can see it in how they dress, how they speak to others and how they treat themselves, be that the food they put in their body, what they drink or the substances they use (from vitamins to drugs). People want to be around positivity, not negativity, and, more times than not, having or not having respect is at the root of that.

There is the misconception that respect has to be earned – and that, therefore, we don't have to give respect until it's earned. I believe the opposite to be true: respect must be given in order for it to be received. This is true whether you are giving respect to yourself or someone else.

The reality is that you should respect your family, your neighbor, the law, all aspects of life and, above all, yourself, because respect is priceless. It's one of the few things a person can't buy.

It may sound unbelievable, but I show respect to everybody I come across. You may find yourself in situations with certain people where you find yourself tested. Even in those times, you can still give respect and receive it in return. I offer some advice below.

You have a **RACIST**, someone who discriminates.

I've learned that the bigots and racists of today were often influenced as children by the bigots and racists of yesterday. Remember what I said about that before? The blame for this type of behavior goes so far back it's saddening. We can't do anything about that. What we can do is carry ourselves with self-respect, which I think was one of the best defenses against racism historically and still is today. Self-respect is displayed in your demeanor and is therefore obvious to others, even those who discriminate. A respectful person knows how to counter the disrespect of a racist by relying on his/her own sense of worth.

A racist does not have self-respect, nor does a racist have respect for others. The most deferential thing you can expect from someone who discriminates is ... nothing. That means if a racist does not give you a disgusted look or stare, does not make indirect or direct gestures, and does not make any offensive comments or statements, that's about the most you can expect from them.

Ask yourself: How can you give respect when there is a void? By not acknowledging the void. You merely have to draw from your own well of self-respect and move on. I've learned that, like a racist, saying nothing at all shows more respect than saying something disrespectful.

> You have a **FOREIGNER**, someone who's allegiance is to another
> country or who belongs to another country.

In reality, we are all foreigners who have met on land that was colonized. Colonization, by nature, goes against respect; therefore, it is disrespectful. To gain back what we have lost, to show genuine respect for all people of foreign backgrounds, we must have self-respect. We must love who we are as individuals, which means being comfortable in one's own skin. If we love ourselves, we can love others. (Think back to the racist here!)

You have **THE RICH**, someone possessing or controlling great wealth.

In some cases, those with great wealth feel they're superior to those who are not as wealthy and can, at times, show little to no respect to those less fortunate. Sometimes, that lack of respect is caused by personal insecurities and/or a suspicion of others. If that's the case, those with wealth need to work on their own self-respect.

Many say that with good fortune comes great responsibilities, which I believe to be true. In other words, those with good fortune need to have a bit more respect for those without. On the other hand, if those less fortunate maintain a bit more self-respect, then the rich would have no choice but to offer respect. It's simple: lack of self-respect brings forth disrespect; increased self-respect brings forth increased respect.

I have learned that if there's one thing rich people love more than money, it's the things in life that are priceless. So, what's more priceless that genuine and true respect? Nothing.

I'd like to mention this: You should never harbor any ill feelings toward those of good fortune or those who are more fortunate than yourself. Those ill feelings will keep you from getting the respect you deserve. Instead, fortunate people should be the motivation you need to pursue your own fortune.

Reminder: Good fortune is based on financial standings. Great fortune is based on respect that stems from self-respect.

You have the **POOR**, someone who is lacking material possessions or whose possessions are inferior in quality and value.

Those who have fortune and those who don't seem to have one thing in common – they have a propensity to disrespect the poor. What I find insane is that nobody seems to be bothered by all this disrespect, yet everyone wants to be respected.

Respect can lift a person's spirits to the point that they can find the courage or inspiration to take steps toward overcoming their misfortune. The poor deserve just as much respect as the next person, and perhaps even more because they live a life so many others couldn't bear.

My belief is that a large percentage of the world is poor at heart and/or in spirit, which is no different than being without fortune. So why not put a stop to all the lack of respect? We must stop being judgmental and start being compassionate.

> You have the **NEIGHBOR**, someone who lives or is located near another, or to be next to; to border.

We should have the utmost respect for our neighbor, regardless of their financial status, race, gender and/or age. We must have consideration for others in order to create and sustain a great community. Nobody is happy in a community where respect for one another is lacking. Knowing that family is related to unity and unity is related to happiness, we should treat our neighbor as our brother – with respect.

We should keep in mind that true respect shines like the sun in the daytime and the moon at night. Common sense says that the best and only true reason to respect others is because everyone wants to be respected. Without respect, there is no loyalty.

I used to ride the coattails of those members of my family who were respected. My own level of self-respect wasn't too high due to my perceived misfortune; this caused me to be less deferential toward others. Growing up, I was aware of needing to be respectful, yet it was only directed toward adults in my family and those whose authority I approved of. My regard for everyone else was very limited – though this was only when I was with my mother. For some strange reason, when I was around my father and his side of the family, my regard for others was higher. When I was with them, I felt that I had to be respected, and therefore I had no reason to be disrespectful. I wasn't consciously aware of this change in my attitude and behavior growing up.

When I was around my mother, I actually felt that people were justified in disrespecting me; yet, with my father, I felt that people had better not dare. Little did I know, this isn't the way to gain true respect.

I had problems accepting my misfortune and, until I knew how to deal with it, my self-esteem would remain low: With low self-esteem comes low self-respect. Therefore, I was prevented from truly respecting others and understanding that an adult is someone who is mature. I wasn't being taken seriously and, even though I reaped the benefits of the respect my family commanded, many viewed me as immature. Eventually, I got tired of being known as "a funny dude", "what-cha call it's son", etc.

If I ever wanted to be respected for who I was, I needed to raise my level of self-respect. Afterwards, I would have to display that self-respect through my actions. Once people saw that I was holding myself with self-respect and giving more respect to others, they seemed to gravitate toward me. To me, there wasn't anything more satisfying than knowing that people respected me for being me. The respect I received from those who were more fortunate motivated me to do better with my life and broaden my horizons. All of a sudden, all kinds of opportunities seemed to be available to me. People were actually listening when I spoke and were willing to assist me in bettering my life, and I whole-heartedly respected them for taking an interest in me. I believe many things good come from showing respect. I'm living proof of it.

03

LOYALTY IS WHAT YOU SHOULD SEEK

LOYALTY:
Faithful adherence to a sovereign, government, leader, cause, etc.

Loyalty is priceless. We know this because wars have been fought over it – wars between nations, wars between families great and small, and street wars with repercussions greater than what caused them to begin with. You know why? Because loyalty is also unconditional. You can't be a little bit disloyal; once that line has been crossed, there is no going back. It's that real. Think about that friend who you trusted completely until one day they up and did something you thought was disloyal. Maybe they didn't stick up for you at work to your boss, or maybe they didn't invite your kid their kid's birthday party when you always invited theirs, or maybe they got with your ex after you broke up with them. How'd you feel after those moments? Not good, probably. You probably also vowed never to be loyal to them again. Your trust was broken, and you were disrespected.

There's that word "respect" again, right?

We can now start to see how respect and loyalty work in tandem with each other. I personally don't think you can have one without the other. You can't be respectful to someone without having some sort of loyalty to them, and you can't be loyal to someone without having some level of respect for them.

So, to achieve and maintain loyalty, you must have respect. It becomes a litmus test to help you choose who and/or what to be loyal to. If a large amount of respect is present, that's a go for loyalty. If respect is low or barely detectable, there's no reason to expend any more of your energy toward being loyal. It's that simple.

Let's put this into practice. How do you know who to be loyal to? In real life, in real time, it can be very difficult to know who is worthy of your loyalty because not everyone appreciates loyalty – not even yours. Rather than spending your time guessing, or having sessions on the phone with your boys, or your momma, or your co-worker discussing whether someone is being loyal to you, you need to take care of yourself. And by that, I mean you should operate your life in a way that demands a high level of unconditional respect *daily* and does not entertain anything less. Make respect a habit. Make respect something like your gold chain, your lotion or even your shoes – something you put on every day. When you leave the house, everybody who sees you knows to treat you with respect because you are consistently wearing it for everyone to see (and you're treating yourself with respect!). Only then, because it is a habit, will you be able to know who is worthy of your loyalty and whose loyalty comes with a price or conditions. That's because your respect will be the constant, unconditional measure – not theirs.

Remember this, though: You have to be righteous – toward yourself and others. You must be strong in your morals and values so that *you* have that strong base of respect within yourself to know when loyalty is even important in a situation. Loyalty is a thing most people mistake for weakness or choose to take advantage of, especially when respect is lacking. However, to me loyalty shows the true strength of a person. Having conviction in what's right and wrong will be your protective armor.

Loyalty needs respect in order to thrive, but where does it come from? By definition, it includes an element of faith and of being faithful. In fact, the definition includes "faithful adherence to sovereign, government, leader, cause, etc."

But how do we know that our faithfulness is warranted?

This brings us to the notion of equality. If I'm faithful to someone (or something), I expect the same in return. I mean, it's very difficult to be loyal to a person, place and/or thing if they aren't loyal to you in return – if they don't treat you as an equal.

And how do we learn equality? At home, with family.

So, going back to the definition of loyalty, we remember it gave us the examples of being faithful to government and leaders, but I think we need to go deeper into the definition. It left out that before being faithful to everything else, you must first be faithful to family. It is at home where we learn our life's lessons. Meaning, if you aren't faithful to the family who nurtured you, then how can you make an outward extension of faithfulness to your government, or your country or a friend? You must start within.

Family itself has many definitions. For me, a family is a social unit, usually consisting of one or two parents and their children. It's typically a group of people with common ancestry. When a family unit is functioning at its best, those parents (or individuals acting as parents) nurture their young with unconditional love, knowledge, wisdom, understanding, food and shelter.

This foundation sets an example for giving and receiving; it should be your safest, most lush place to be loyal, because it has given you the framework to exercise loyalty. If there is an emergency, who do you call? Family. When you are in dire need of assistance, whether it is money or a shoulder to cry on, who do you call? Family. When the world gives you a cold shoulder, who is there for you? Family.

Personally, I believe it's a crime to have more loyalty to any other person, place or thing than you have for your family. There's no justification for it.

Loyalty is the bond that makes family what it is and what keeps family together. Without it, we are nothing more than relatives – distant relations who aren't close.

I strongly believe that if you wish to prosper in life, you must have loyalty to family. Loyalty to family means that you are grounded in the right things, for the right reasons, at the right times. This will help you maintain respect, regardless of situations and people who have little to no respect to offer you in return.

If we treated each other like family, we would be in a better place. We would feed one another, protect one another, and love one another unconditionally. We would foster loyalty to one another.

We would lead more righteous lives.

There's one important family member I left out, and that's our Maker. We are all the children of a Higher Power, our Maker. If we have loyalty to our Higher Power, the one who makes us all family that are connected as one, then it shouldn't be so hard to be loyal and, therefore, to respectful to one another.

We see now how important loyalty is: loyalty brings unity. It brings us that much closer to achieving a P.L.U.S.H. Lyfe.

CONFESSION

There's no doubt that I consider myself to be a loyal person – now. But I would say that there was a time when I, too, misunderstood what it meant to be loyal. It was years of heartache and pain, not to mention trials and tribulations, before I realized the difference between loyalty and selfishness. I say selfishness because so many people, including myself, did and have done things solely for personal benefit. Loyalty is selfless and comes from respect for someone and something without expecting to be rewarded in any way. These days, the only thing I hope to get for being loyal is loyalty in return and nothing else. At one point in time, I felt there was no need to be loyal when nobody appreciated the loyalty I displayed. Yet, in the long run, I learned that if I remained a respectable, loyal person, I would receive the strength needed to prosper in life.

I wasn't always aware that true loyalty is built upon respect. I also wasn't aware that a person who chose to take advantage of my loyalty had absolutely no respect for me. In fact, I just figured being loyal wasn't such a great thing, because it opened the door to let people take advantage of me. I mean, it's not like I was unaware of how the world wants to work – that while I should be a person of respect and loyalty, I should also be aware that there are people who prey on that respect and loyalty. At points, I knew that people were taking advantage of me. Therefore, for a long time my attitude was, "Fuck the world before the world fucks me!" Instead of just taking my time to use my knowledge and understand the signs that separate a loyal person from a disloyal one, I held on to that attitude, and it caused me to miss out on receiving true respect, loyalty, strength and above all – happiness.

What I realize now is that when my loyalty was to my family and those who I considered family, my life was better off. When my loyalty was to the streets and my street friends, my life was chaotic. Now when I say, "who I consider family," I mean those people who I would invite over to dinner with my family, or, when I was a kid, who I'd invite to sleep over. By "street friends" I mean those who had no chance of meeting any of my family, let alone being invited into my home. My loyalty is now to my loved ones and those loved ones consist of honorable men, women and children. Remember, with unconditional love comes loyalty.

I've learned that it is respect that rewards being respectful, and loyalty that rewards being loyal. The reward for being both respectful and loyal is unity, which is true strength. *It takes a lot of strength to be a respectable and loyal person; it is easier to be disrespectful and disloyal. That's so easy that a child can do it.*

It was hard for me to understand that. I had to learn that, until I changed how I viewed things, I would never truly prosper. And I would first have to take some difficult steps.

No matter what, I have to respect that not everyone will walk the path I walk. This goes for everyone I cross paths with, from my family to my associates, and even to the ideology of the country I live in and the ideas of our people. I refuse to allow myself to become a disrespectful and disloyal individual due to those who can't or won't appreciate mine or anyone else's respect and loyalty.

This is free will and it is from here that I now operate.

04

WHEN TRUE STRENGTH IS THE ANSWER

STRENGTH:
The state or quality of being strong; the power to resist attack.

Strength is defined as the quality of being strong. I often think about
being strong. I think, "What does that even mean?" So often, we tell
people to "Be strong!" when they're going through a tough time and
dealing with a death in the family or a financial loss. We demand the same
thing of ourselves. We force ourselves to be strong in front of our friends,
our boss or our kids. I think we need to rework this mantra; it might be
better for us to just say, "Hey man, have strength!" Why? Because to be
strong, to me, is to have strength.

Yet, what is strength?

Strength falls into three categories, external, eternal and internal. We
need to be resilient in all three areas as strength is an important key
to the pursuit of peace, love, unity, success and happiness on earth, or
achieving P.L.U.S.H.

External strength is physical strength, eternal is spiritual strength and
internal strength relates to our mental strength. Each of these three
areas need attention and input from us to be the best person we can be.
If you are working on yourself – which I hope is the reason you picked
up this book – you might be wondering, "Where do I start?" You should
work from the inside out, based upon this order of importance: internal,
eternal and then external. Think about it. If you have a strong base from
the inside, your outside will have a greater chance of being strong too.
You can see how the relationship between the three buckets of strength
works in a circle, which shouldn't be broken; for example, it's always good
to maintain your physical (external) strength while seeking to enhance
your mental (internal) and spiritual (eternal) strength. This practice and
process will make you strong.

Because I'm a man, it would perhaps appear obvious that external strength would be extremely important in my life – maybe even the most important of the three. I've found this not to be the case! In fact, external strength isn't anywhere near as important as internal or eternal strength. External strength is only good for physical tasks and nothing more. Yet, if we want to go deep with this analogy, I offer this: that same physical task can be handled with internal strength and eternal strength. I say this because to achieve something you must *think* it to be so mentally and then you must *believe* it to be so spiritually, thereby allowing you to physically accomplish anything. I live by this thinking.

In fact, I'm a firm believer that it takes more internal and eternal strength to do right than it does to do wrong. Honestly, if you are not strong internally and eternally, you are destined to face numerous trials and tribulations. Nobody has time for that. Now, how does strength play into us achieving P.L.U.S.H.? Let's take a look.

Strength is an important key to P.L.U.S.H. because it relies upon and encourages unity. Yes, we have to be strong individuals, but true strength is in numbers. Here's my proof. See if you agree or disagree:

- It takes one person to start a war, yet it takes many people to fight it.
- It takes one person to commit a crime, yet it takes many people to serve justice.
- It takes one person to come up with an idea, yet it takes many people to make it a reality.
- It takes a man and woman to make a child, yet it takes a village to raise that child.

We must work together to make change; we must work together to solve problems; and we must work together to merely exist. We must be united.

41

Think of the phrase, "United we stand, divided we fall", a sentiment which appears throughout the Bible, politics and everywhere in between. Strength first must begin with us as individuals, then within our individual families, and then within our community. It only builds from there, radiating out to how we exist within a city, a state, a country and finally how we exist in the whole world. It's safe to assume that this phrase could mean that no matter how strong we may be physically, if we aren't just as strong internally and eternally, we will weaken slowly but surely – not just us as individuals, but also in the infrastructures through which we relate.

Building upon what we've discussed so far, I'd like to take this notion of strength a step further with you – to understand where it comes from. In earlier chapters I explained how respect and loyalty are symbiotic: You can't have one without the other. Together, as a combined force, respect and loyalty produce a state of equality and honesty. When we experience respect (peace) and loyalty (love), we are operating in a fortified environment that is surrounded by equality and honesty. This environment, like oxygen, provides us with strength. We need all of those pieces of respect, loyalty, equality and honesty in order to thrive and to nourish our eternal, internal and external strength to make us strong human beings. I'll break it down even further. Respect (peace) and loyalty (love) will give us the strength (unity) to work together to make the money (success) that will allow us to provide for one another.

CONFESSION

By the time I began to realize that true strength consisted of internal, eternal external power, I was around thirty-one years of age. Although it may have appeared to me growing up that strength was in numbers alone, due to a lack of true strength those numbers slowly began to dwindle. My focus was solely on external strength. To be truthful, I had no clue about internal or eternal strength, which blinded me to realizing that the unity that had formed in my life only existed within a group seeking external power and strength. It wasn't long before that group began to divide and fall. Yet, at the time, I was ignorant to our impending fate. For a long time, I believed I had the best judgement when it came to choosing the people I should surround myself with. Now I realize that I probably had the worst judgement (or simply poor judgement) – and that's because I wasn't sure of the type of person I was or wanted to be.

It's ironic that we tend to expect strength or unity when we have no idea what the key to achieving such strength and bringing forth unity really is. This goes back to respect, honesty, loyalty and trust, all of which are important in obtaining true strength within the unit. It is the eternal, internal and external strength that makes our unity impossible to divide and conquer. These days, when I look back at how I was and the frame of mind I was in, I see where I went wrong. My first mistake was not knowing or understanding that life is not only about me. That it's about my family and, although our family unit may have had its trials and tribulations, we remained a family. As I grew older, my life became about doing better than how things had been for me growing up; I only saw the external misfortunes that had befallen me and was focused on moving beyond those misfortunes. My pursuit for external strength, which I realized also was socially motivated, ultimately weakened my internal and eternal strengths, which had actually been deeply instilled within me.

I realized my core strength was never an issue growing up. My internal and eternal strength was solid. It only was my external strength that became weak. Since most of society is concerned with external strength, the emphasis on it caused it to become the most important marker of success in my life. Over time, I came to believe it was pointless to be concerned with the morals (internal strength) and values (eternal strength) that were instilled in me as a child. It was that belief that caused me to live a dishonest lifestyle, which consisted of lying, cheating and stealing – in addition to being untrustworthy, disrespectful and disloyal. It got to the point where I'd do practically anything for that external strength and social satisfaction.

It was long afterwards when I became aware that I was losing my internal and eternal strength. Along with that, I found myself alone because my actions and ways were the opposite of those who exercised strong morals and values, those who possessed true strength. They didn't enjoy seeing me weaken myself, and they refused to allow my false sense of strength plague their unity. I wasn't aware of how much pain my family had endured because of my disregard for the strong morals and values they instilled in me. Still, they patiently waited and hoped for my weakened morals and values to regain their strength.

Just imagine this scenario:

I turned to the streets and the street dwellers, to people who I thought were respectable or friends. I had to because everything in the streets is territorial. You have to belong to something or you won't survive. Now, all of us were out to make it big and be the supreme team – a formidable unit consisting of trust, respect and loyalty. There were some who were internally stronger than others, which meant they had big plans. There were some who were stronger externally, which meant they had access to capital (money and drugs). Then, there were the very few who were eternally stronger; they believed it was destiny for them to succeed, but they just did not or could not see how or when. Some, if not all, of us were strong in two of the three areas. Ironically, however, the area where I thought I was strong, I wasn't. One thing was true, we "the team" or "unit", as we called ourselves, had plans of doing big things to better ourselves and we formed a bond. The unit was like the military. You were assigned to your people and you were obligated to them – sometimes for life.

There was one thing wrong. We all sought external strength and that became a conflict of interest. Still, for the sake of the unit we endured one another; meanwhile, however, we were also waiting for that opportunity to abandon it. It seemed that this unity wasn't formed around trust, respect or loyalty after all. In fact, those who were internally strong didn't agree with the direction of the team, so there was no loyalty. Those who were eternally strong didn't believe in their hearts that everyone was indeed all for one, so their trust level was extremely low. As for those who were externally strong, they had little to no respect for the others because of their external strength. After everything was all said and done, we all divided and we all fell, some sooner than others and some harder than the rest.

The worst part is that when I fell, I was so detached from my family, who still truly cared about me, that I couldn't even make it back to them for help. My true strength wasn't associated with those I was in the streets with, but those I'd left behind for the streets.

The best part is my true strength never left me, but instead just waited for me to return. My family understood how society and social pressure could mislead someone like myself. In fact, my uncle was the one who always used to tell me to stand for something. I spent a lot of time not standing for anything, but I never forgot what he told me. And that was a good thing, because I finally understood what was real. The question back then had been whether I would understand before it was too late. Thankfully, it only would have been too late if I had died.

When I first wrote this book, I was incarcerated and was facing twenty years in a federal prison. This inspired me to reflect on my life and life in general. Although I might not have been focused on writing a book prior to my incarceration, I was definitely beginning to understand that I needed to change prior to it. So, I've not only talked the talk; I also walked the walk every day of my incarceration. I choose to deal with respect and in return I receive respect, which also comes with loyalty. Those who truly respected my pursuit of P.L.U.S.H. received my loyalty, and I made it a point to not abuse the loyalty of the weak. The unity formed while incarcerated was strong – although it was tested often. But, for the most part, it was strengthened by every test. The unity formed was not founded on money, drugs or brawn, but instead trust, honesty and equality. We spent every day strengthening each other internally, eternally and externally. At that time, when I didn't know what my future would hold beyond the institution that incarcerated me, I vowed to walk the walk without concern for all the days that were to come and to dedicate myself to the pursuit of P.L.U.S.H.

05

IN MONEY
WE TRUST?

MONEY:

Something generally accepted as a medium of exchange, a measure of value, or a means of payment: such as officially coined or stamped metal currency, money of account, paper money.

Money is an object that causes much controversy and confusion due to immorality and the poor values most people have. If morals and values are not founded on equality and honesty, then money can and will become the root of all evil.

In 1956, President Dwight D. Eisenhower signed a law that officially proclaimed "In God We Trust" as our official motto. That same year, our country even had the audacity to mandate our paper money be printed with the phrase. (The phrase had been on U.S. coins since the Civil War.)

In God we trust? It's as if they were implying that money should be looked to in the same way one looks to God as a savior. If so, then there is no possible excuse on this planet for why money wouldn't become the root of all evil – we're going about it all wrong. Money is not a savior to be worshipped. How about in peace we trust, or in love we trust? This money that's stamped with "In God We Trust" is being used for all that is not righteous.

In God We Trust

People care more about being in the million-dollar club than they do the millions of hungry, sick and homeless. The sad truth is that not one of those wanna-be millionaires would be able to survive a week, a month or a year without everything money provides. I'm sure almost everybody has seen the 1983 movie *Trading Places* with Eddie Murphy and Dan Aykroyd. (If not, then I highly recommend it.) The movie is about a reversal of fortune and really does a great job of showing human nature and how we treat those with money and, more importantly, those without. It also entertains what low levels we will stoop to while trying to get money or keep it. Really, the movie shows the power money has and the power it has over us.

Having money is okay. I'm not saying we shouldn't have or want money. It is how we regard it that matters. When money is given too much value in our life, it's no longer okay. Once money is given that power and value above and beyond everything else then it becomes the root of all evil.

How do we give it power? I think we give it power by how we use it. These days, it is being used for more wrong than right.

More and more I'm left to believe that more money – billions in fact – is spent on promoting violence, sex, drugs and cigarettes than is spent on promoting and producing peace, love, unity, success and happiness on earth.

It's a moral fact. Money is misused. It is rarely used to benefit the people as a whole.

Instead, it is used primarily to benefit the chosen ones. Let's look at peace. Peace benefits people as a whole. War benefits the chosen few who wage it.

I believe war to be one of the most expensive things the world spends money on. Yet, past, present and future wars are all supposedly in the name of peace. It seems that it might be a lot cheaper to search for peace without the use of war, since war only provokes more wars. Or is it money? Is money (i.e., another country's resources, be they people, land or oil) the reason we go to war in the first place? It's something to think about. Think about this too: how much money is spent to prepare for wars? First, we pay for the weapons to be made, then to train different people to use them in battle, and finally, when the time comes, we pay to go to battle. Not to mention all the secretive stuff being paid for, nor the money being used to rebuild those whose lives were ruined in a country we paid to destroy. Regardless of how we may justify these useless tactics that cost us so dearly in so many ways, is it truly worth it? The billions and even trillions of dollars could have simply been used to ensure peace and freedom.

What would it be like if money was used for world peace and not for wars of the world?

What if we spent money on love and equality? Once again, love and equality benefit the people as a whole. Greed and lack benefit the chosen.

Let's look at our prison system. Our prison system is privatized. That means private individuals and corporations greedily benefit from the economic return afforded by the prison system.

It's sad how much money goes into housing non-violent offenders and those who commit petty crimes. Yet not nearly the same amount of money goes into housing those who can't afford housing and who don't commit any offenses. My point is not to say that a crime should go unpunished, but I believe we need to focus on prevention and not the cure.

Jails and detention centers are built continuously without any problems, while homeless shelters and soup kitchens are struggling to remain open or are being forced to close. Supposedly it is just too costly to take care of these people; meanwhile, it is a fact that it costs much more to house criminals of all offense levels. Don't forget to factor in health care. Mind you, the soup kitchens and shelters don't offer the medical coverage that is afforded to those who commit all levels of criminal offenses, and that expense is being paid for by almost everyone who pays taxes. We've got to ask, why not let all that money be used to focus on the needy? With this type of reallocation of funds those who are helped off the street or provided shelter could , at the very least, become productive members of society.

Money should be directed to the homeless, the sick and the hungry. This would be a step toward preventing future criminal behaviors instead of provoking them. Most criminal offenses are committed due to hunger, poverty and medical conditions and yet we prefer to pay a higher price for the cure. Where is the logic when we reward the criminals and punish those who struggle to survive and commit few to no crimes?

It is obvious that we have the means to right our wrongs, but that's just too easy – or is it that "United We Stand" is more costly than "Divided We Fall?" This is exactly what the people of the world are saying when they invest in prisons, jails and detention centers instead of shelters and medical facilities for those in need.

In Equality We Trust

Equality and honesty build trust. If we place our trust here, rather than in money, we begin to build P.L.U.S.H.

True strength and happiness are free of a price tag. If indeed we trust God, then money should not play a major role in our lives, especially since it plays a major role in so much that is evil. Only those who indeed trust in God and who honestly believe in equality will use money without letting money use them. They will remember that money is not worth more than family, loved ones, respect, love, peace or anything else of real importance.

CONFESSION

I've got to admit that I was not in the right frame of mind when it came to dealing with money – not to mention the route I took to making money, which was not worth the risk in the end. It's believed that the key to happiness is having an abundance of money. This way of thinking has so many people, including the previous version of myself, doing almost any and everything to make a lot of it. Thinking like that also makes it difficult to differentiate between our needs and our wants or desires. It is this frame of mind that caused the trials and tribulations in my life, which in turn affected those I cared a great deal about and loved dearly. The sad thing is that I was so addicted to making money that I pushed all my morals and values to the side. Now I realize that pushing morals and values aside makes it practically impossible to achieve happiness in life.

The worst part is how the adage that "money brings power and respect" is constantly promoted. Well, I beg to differ with that, especially since I too used to believe it was true.

I went many years having an abundance of money, only to achieve no greater power nor respect for it. In fact, the little bit of power and respect I did have did not come from how much money I had. What I did come to realize is that without some discipline and good morals and values, money can be the root of all evil. Though I had money, I was not happy within myself. Sustaining my lifestyle was incredibly expensive, which meant that I had to work even longer and harder just to maintain it. This also meant that things I would have rather spent my time doing had to be put on hold. Those things consisted of spending time with my loved ones, traveling and being able to achieve any of my short- or long-term goals.

It was madness and insanity to have been living beyond my means while still believing I was going to be able to accomplish anything that I had set out to accomplish.

I remember growing up not having the newest or latest things a kid could want, but back then it didn't mean much to me. I had friends who were not concerned with what I did or didn't have because, when it was all said and done, we had fun. That fun consisted of everything from sports to girls – none of which demanded having money. It was obvious that some families had more than others, yet it was not something we cared about as kids.

Deep down, I never chose my friends based on their financial status, at least not consciously. I say this because when I think about it, I was so determined to make money that I only associated with those who could make that happen. I associated with those who could help me in my quest for money; those in the drug game who could sell, buy or bring product back to me. That was it.

I had friends, or should I say people I thought were my friends, who traded in respect and loyalty for money. Although I remained respectful and loyal to them, they still betrayed me just so they could gain financially. Their respect and loyalty were sold for a few dollars and their morals and values were pawned for some change. My anger about this resulted in me doing the same thing in retaliation. For years I've justified my own madness by pointing to other's insanity, and them to mine, but no matter what, at the root of it all was money. I saw money turn people into murderers, who at one point in time were not very different from me.

I would like to clarify that while I saw how money changes people, I'm not blaming money. Remember, money is an object, a piece of paper or metal. I am instead blaming the people who give money such an extraordinary value. Even I was one of those people who gave money too much power in my life. If not for the tough times I was unfortunate to go through, I would never have taken the time to see how twisted my thinking was.

Here's the thing: I had been selling drugs or otherwise associated with drugs from age fifteen. I went to jail at age thirty-three. That's almost twenty years of my life pursuing money. It got even deeper at one point. Remember how I told you I'd wake up to hookers at the breakfast table as a teen? Well, my brother's friend realized we had addicts right in the house! We could make money inside our own home, with even having to go anywhere. I saw a lot of women (and men) do a lot of things for drugs. It let me know that everything has a price.

These days, I have a better way of thinking when it comes to dealing with money. I've come to the realization that money was not the reason my loved ones loved me or cared about me. So, with that thought in mind, I'm satisfied with not having an abundance of money and plan on strengthening my morals and values instead. Let me make one thing very clear though: I'm not saying we don't need money. My uncle, the one who told me to stand for something? I watched him die from AIDS because the treatment he needed was too expensive. He served in the military as a man loyal to his country – a country that didn't show him the same loyalty in turn. I needed to get that out because I want you all to know where I'm coming from.

Still. I can honestly say that I'm happy to be free from the way I used to think and how I used to behave. I'm happy and it has nothing to do with the amount of money I have in the bank. Also, I sleep good at night now.

I know I'm not going to get robbed by some crackhead or somebody out looking for loyalty, and my door isn't going to get kicked in by either, nor by some cop out looking for me or for glory. I am at peace, and I want you to be too.

06

REDEFINING POWER

POWER:
Having great influence, force or authority; a nation having influence on another nation.

When people think about power, or what it means to be powerful, they think about control. For example, when someone has a lot of money, we think that person is powerful. We believe this because we see they can control others with their money. Therefore, we think, "If I have a lot of money, people will do as I say! I will be powerful."

This line of thinking is flawed. When we think this way, we are putting the emphasis and the importance on the wrong thing. In this case, the wrong thing is money.

I want to introduce you to something I have been thinking about and that is the concept of universal power. Universal power exists irrespective of money, imposed force, surrounding conditions, deception, dishonor or treachery. Instead, it is simply based upon honesty and equality. I've concluded that those who have been and/or are fortunate to be in the position of power, often abuse it – even when they may believe this abuse is for a good cause. I do believe that there is no way to abuse universal power because it is founded in honesty and equality.

If we are honest and practice equality, we will gain power. We will be powerful. Here's why:

When we focus on the wrong thing to give us power, we ultimately are focusing on the concept of control. We feel that we must control something or someone in order to make them do what we want. The problem here is that using control or using force takes away a person's free will. For example, my boss holds a certain power over me, right? If

I want to get paid, I have to do what my boss says. If my boss *tells* me to work overtime, he is taking away my free will to say, "Yes, I can work those extra hours" or "No, I can't work those extra hours."

By taking away my free will (my ability to act at my own discretion), he's technically not treating me with equality. And, if he's telling me to work overtime because he needs to make up for losses that were a result of his mismanagement, then he's not being honest either. He is making me accountable for his mistakes.

As his employee, if I feel powerless and like my ability to choose is being taken away, I'm going to react in some kind of way. For a lot of us, including me, that reaction includes stress or anger, which will result in quitting, arguing or having a bad attitude and not trusting our boss any longer. Now I'm a "bad" employee, and I'm working in a toxic environment.

If my boss *asked* me to work overtime and also explained his situation with a sense of honesty, equality and even loyalty, he is going to retain a higher and difference sense of power, because I will respect him and offer him loyalty in return. These are the things that create and build power beyond the kind that money can buy.

Therefore, nothing of greatness can come or can last from power that's based upon money and/or force. This type of deception only brings about loss – loss of respect, loyalty, strength, success, freedom and even wealth.

I offer you this:

The **Power** of true <u>Peace</u> is Freedom.
The **Power** of true <u>Love</u> is Strength.
The **Power** of true <u>Unity</u> is Loyalty.
The **Power** of true <u>Success</u> is Wealth.
The **Power** of true <u>Happiness</u> is Respect.
The **Power** of <u>P.L.U.S.H.</u> is Righteousness.

If you want to live righteously, if you want to live with true power, then I ask you to practice peace, love, unity, success and happiness. When you live your life within these guidelines and are *influential* in these ways, you will experience power! You will give and receive a sense of freedom. You will feel strong, and you will provide strength to others. You will become loyal, and others will be loyal to you. You will gain wealth and others will want to share their wealth with you. You will willingly give respect and you will receive immense respect in return.

When the majority of people in the world obtain universal power, then P.L.U.S.H. on earth is going to be possible! If you're not sure where to start, I suggest starting with the basics of honesty and equality.

This is my theory. It is based on living and learning as I live.

CONFESSION

When it comes to the word "power" many people either misunderstand it or have misused the bit of power they supposedly have. I, too, had a complete misunderstanding of the word "power" and what true power brings about.

At first, I was led to believe that brute strength gave a person power, which in reality is far from true, especially if it's respect that a person seeks. Then I was led to believe that having a lot of money gave a person power, which is also far from true if respect is what a person seeks. Yet I was so eager to be respected that I did whatever it took to obtain lots of money. Let me be the first to tell you that things didn't always turn out the way I expected.

I decided to reevaluate my understanding of the word power, taking a much broader perspective. This also meant that I had to accept that my values were tainted due to my misunderstandings. I had to accept that I'd been misinformed for most of my adult life.

To change, I asked myself, "What do I truly expect to gain once I have achieved power?" What I came to realize is that to obtain power I first needed to decide if it was external, internal and/or eternal power that I was seeking. External power I defined as brute strength and/or money. Internal power included knowledge and wisdom. Eternal power consisted of being trustworthy and honest, honorable and understanding.

I have come to the conclusion that I would rather have eternal power. To achieve the status of having eternal power meant I must first be respectable and loyal. Embodying those qualities brings about all the elements that create eternal power.

Many people do not know how to accept nor appreciate being respected for their loyalty. I found that many people, like me, were also led to believe that respect and loyalty came from money and/or brute strength. From what I have studied, this has been a misconception that has played a major role in the lives of many people, for many years. In response, I see the need to focus on opening my mind and the minds of others to a more reasonable understanding of "power."

Having power seems pointless if it isn't everlasting. I've incorporated this theory in my everyday life, and it has proven itself to be righteous. This theory has changed my understanding of power and how not to misuse it – however much or little I possess in a situation.

I believe this theory will bring about everlasting power once it is incorporated into the lives of my loved ones, and the lives of their loved ones, and so on.

07

THE COST OF FREEDOM

FREEDOM:

Being free, independence, civil or political liberty, exemption from obligation, discomfort.

> **Freedom** *is the right of enjoying all the privileges of membership and/or citizenship.*
> **Freedom** *is the right to unrestricted use and/or full access.* **Freedom** *is nothing but a meaningless word if it is not based on* **True Equality**.

Of all the principles I've mentioned thus far, freedom is the clearest and simplest. It is the state of being free. I believe it is our right as human beings to be free. However, with freedom comes great responsibility and those responsibilities are being honest, trustworthy, knowledgeable, wise and divine. When we strive to embody these responsibilities, I consider this process, or really journey, to be a form of mental evolution.

The freedom we seek is within our grasp, but only if we desire it. It takes consistent dedication.

While freedom requires a dedicated approach to your own mental evolution, it's worth mentioning that freedom does not exist without equality. True, unbiased, unadulterated equality. Why? Because equality is needed for people to experience peace, love, unity, success and happiness.

Here is another way to ponder the effects of true equality:

With **True Equality** *comes* **Respect**.
With **True Equality** *comes* **Loyalty**.
With **True Equality** *comes* **Strength**.
With **True Equality** *comes* **Wealth**.
With **True Equality** *comes* **Freedom**.

Is your mind ready to be free?

CONFESSION

Freedom is not only something I took for granted, but also something I watched being slowly taken away. In the year prior to my incarceration, I didn't have a clue about how priceless freedom is. While I'd been incarcerated before, I never took time out to reflect on my life as a whole and the role freedom played in it.

I had a problem. I felt trapped by what society was giving me, which seemed like a big plate of nothing. What I've come to realize is that so many people, including myself, look for a cure to a problem instead of how to prevent it. I had ways to prevent feeling this way; I had the option to make different choices in my life. Instead, I looked to other things as ways to cure my problem. The sad thing is this mentality is being passed down from generation to generation. It's this way of thinking that had me sabotaging my own freedom, which is insane to say the least. I've come to recognize this sabotage as mental slavery, which is just as bad (if not worse) than the institution of human slavery this country was built upon. I believe this to be so because mental slavery conflicts with the power of free will. It is that power of free will that supplies freedom to whomever chooses to utilize it.

When I wasn't incarcerated physically, I was still incarcerated mentally and because of it, true freedom was not an option. As a person living the street life and seeking respect and money, I did things that, in all reality, prevented me from achieving what I set out to find. I was searching for freedom from what lack of money, lack of power and lack of respect had given me – a void. I wanted to be free of feeling that void and being ruled by it. Being ruled by lack. What I found instead were chains that bound me to fear. I was running from the law. At the same time, I had to limit my area of movement in fear of those out for my riches having access to me. I had no freedom; I was caged like an animal.

Here is something I wrote back then: *It would appear now that I am fighting to be able to do those simple things in life that I spent years fighting against. The only thing different this time around is that I've been able to break free mentally. I am able to utilize the power of free will and it has helped me in more ways than one.*

The existence of this book is a prime example of how I chose free will and chose to do something with myself other than being trapped by things that no longer served me. I've used the freedom to write this book, the freedom to respect others as well as myself, the freedom to be honest at all times, the freedom to be loyal and the freedom to call on the strength needed to not compromise my loyalty. Finally, I am free from allowing money to determine my success in life.

08

YOU CAN'T BE
A LITTLE BIT HONEST

HONESTY:

The quality or condition of being honest; integrity. Truthfulness; sincerity.

The other day, my four-year-old son ran into my office asking for yet another popsicle. I'd asked him if he had finished cleaning up his room. I knew he hadn't, but I just wanted to hear how he was going to handle this situation. His lips were already orange, and he was thirsty for more sugar. He said, "Yes" that he had finished cleaning his room. Now, I'm not one to lose my temper with my son. I have worked really hard on that. I want to teach him that there are calmer ways to communicate rather than a whole lot of screaming and yelling. So, while my *abuelita* would have tore my ass up for lying about something like this, I chose not to. I said, "I'm going to give you one more chance to tell me the truth. Did you finish cleaning up your room?" He shook his curly little head, "No." I asked him why he lied to me, and he said what I already knew to be his truth, "I wanted the popsicle." I sat him down and explained to him why telling the truth and being honest were the most important things he needed to do right now.

Honesty is one of the main elements of integrity that I instill and *nurture* in my son, because without honesty, we have nothing. Honesty is the foundation to respect, loyalty, strength, money, power and freedom. It does not add up any other way.

Honesty is one of my favorite things to talk about. It is what separates the good from the bad, right from wrong, and success from failure. It's that simple. Honesty is being whole and complete, being free from duplicity, and being upright, genuine and fair. You can't be a little bit honest; you can't be a little bit dishonest. You are either honest and you tell the truth, or you aren't.

Like many philosophers, I tend to believe that honesty cannot be subjected to conditions; it must be unconditional. So, while my son didn't want to intentionally lie to me, he wanted the popsicle more. He used conditions to circumvent the truth.

I am not a perfect man. I am not one now and I certainly wasn't in the past. What I've come to learn is that you cannot be a person of respect if you are dishonest. You cannot be a person of loyalty if you are dishonest. You cannot be a person of equality if you are dishonest. You cannot be a person of freedom if you are dishonest. You cannot be a person of peace if you are dishonest.

You cannot be a person of God or be at one with your higher power if you are dishonest. Honesty is the root of all that is great and righteous, all that is divine.

It is up to us to live righteously, to be honest, and to take measures in how we live our lives so that we are not in positions that later force us to be dishonest. Learn from my son; if he had cleaned is room like he was supposed to, he would not have had to lie to get to a small piece of happiness.

CONFESSION

I must admit that I wasn't the most honest person growing up as a child. There was a point in my life when I told lies for reasons I can't explain to this day. It came to a point where I actually convinced myself that my lies were justified. Sometimes, I actually believed there were no lies, if that makes any sense at all. Yet as I grew older, most lies came back around to bite me in the butt. They exposed the truth of the matter. They exposed me. When others saw me as a dishonest person, they distanced themselves from me.

There's one story I remember. It was Christmas Eve, and we were at my grandmother's house, which was full of people. The kids were upstairs with no adults. We snuck outside to play in the snow. We knew we weren't supposed to be out there and had promised to stay upstairs in the house. Well, we were out there like fools and jumping from the stoop in the neighbor's yard. I slipped and *whop!* I fell. I had to go into the house, stand there holding my bleeding cheek and explain how I lied about staying in the house. My uncle was the one who saw me first, before everybody else had. He knew I was about to lie, so he took me himself to the hospital – on the bus. I had to get stitches and everything. Even though I was a liar, he still took care of me.

As I did and said things that showed and proved I was dishonest, I didn't understand that my actions had diminished the trust others had for me. I lost the respect of my friends and my loved ones. I was the type of kid who would steal money out of purses for lunch money, hustle family for cash, all of it. I experienced a domino effect. Once trust and respect were gone, equality followed after. I was seen as less-than, below them. That all led to my loss of freedom as well – mental and physical.

I was a bad liar. By the time I began the realize that I was a bad liar, I had also decided that it was time for me to accept responsibility for my ways and actions. I did this by being truthful. I stopped telling new lies and I did my best to clean up old lies with the truth. I've come to realize that there is no need for lies and that being truthful is so liberating. I found it to be a hassle to concoct a perfect lie, if there is such a thing. A lie, whether it be a good lie (believable) or a bad lie (unbelievable), takes up too much time and energy. Plus, I would have to remember each and every lie, especially if I had a relationship with the person(s) I lied to. Lying is incredibly exhausting.

It dawned on me that 99.8% of the time I lied was when I was scared and/ or did something wrong. Now, logically speaking, I would have had prior knowledge that what I was doing or what I was about to do was wrong. Therefore, I should not have been afraid to accept responsibility for my ways or actions. I mean, if it scares me and I am worried about getting into trouble, why commit the act in the first place? If I choose to commit the act of something that scares or worries me, then does it truly scare or worry me?

As I grew wiser it became obvious that honesty is indeed the best policy. Not just for me, but for everyone involved with me. This meant I would not be willing to be an accomplice to someone else's lies. I also had to change my ways and actions because they speak louder than my words. And I found that when all three coincide with one another the feeling is priceless.

I know that ever since I started dealing with honesty on a daily basis, my life improved tremendously. It is the key to P.L.U.S.H.

09
EQUALITY DOESN'T COME FOR FREE

EQUALITY:

Having the same rights, abilities, rank. The state or quality of being equal. Of the same quantity, size, value, treatment all equally without regard to race, sex, finance, etc.

Equality brings about power, freedom, strength, loyalty, respect and P.L.U.S.H. on earth. However, for this statement to be true, this has to be something everybody believes in and that means disregarding those things we use to make people unequal like race, sex, finances, etc.

This equality we seek is not as farfetched as some may want us to believe. If some people would be willing to relinquish the power they have over others, we would be closer to equality. If some people would treat others with respect, we would be closer to equality. If some people would practice love and unity, rather than hate and separation, we would be closer to living a life that includes a broader spectrum of equality.

I don't think this is so hard. We must only want it to be so. I want you to think about this: If you are in a position of power, look at your ways and actions. How are you treating others? For example, if you are a boss with employees, are you treating your employees with respect? Are you paying them what they deserve? Are you speaking to them in a way that is honest, empowering and that shows loyalty for their service? Change begins with us. The first step is that we must desire equality over power, wealth, strength and respect. We must also desire it for others in the same way we desire equality for ourselves. It's like respect; if we give respect, we earn respect. If you are coming out of the gas station and someone else is coming in, do you hold the door for that person? Do you step aside and allow them to come in first, or do you bum-rush past them and let the door slam, leaving them to open it for themselves? Your ways and actions right there demonstrated to that person that you believe you are more important than they are; that they are below you and must wait for you to pass. Is that acting in a way of equality? I don't think so.

I've got one more example for you. If you are running the streets, my first question is: Why? Why are you doing what you are doing, for real? The next question is: How are you conducting yourself? Are your actions creating an environment of equality or are you spending 99.8% of your time fighting for it?

The truth of the matter is that our way of life is not that of true equality. Sad as it is, true equality is not attainable on this earth. We can't eradicate all levels of inequality in this lifetime. What we can do is work to make our own corners of the earth better. Just one block, one household, one moment at a time.

Equality is peace (respect), love (loyalty), unity (strength), success (money/wealth), happiness (power & freedom). Equality stems from honesty and trust, which should be exercised at all times without conditions. Equality is having the same privileges, status and rights; being impartial, just and equitable.

CONFESSION

In 2016, I worked my ass off at a warehouse job. I was working in appliances, doing loading and taking inventory. After a while, I really mastered my job. I understood the mechanics of making the warehouse run smoothly. I wanted to move up. I started shadowing my supervisor, who was also my union rep. Years passed. I wasn't moving up. I even learned the computer management system. Finally, I was promoted. Soon, it became pretty clear that I had a new title, but no new responsibilities. I was babysitter for the guys on the floor. I didn't have the same responsibilities a manager is supposed to have. I couldn't hire or fire, and I was not invited to any managerial meetings despite holding the title, "Logistics Manager". It wasn't equal; I wasn't being treated equally or with fairness. I wasn't the same type of manager that my supervisor had been. The thing was, I knew the dynamics of how things were being run. I understood what needed to be done, so I figured that if I worked hard, I'd be able to show them different – that I deserved to be treated with a higher level of managerial respect. Well, that didn't happen. They kept asking me to do more, but didn't acknowledge my experience, knowledge or work ethic.

After a while, I couldn't deal with it. I couldn't accept anything less than equality; they weren't going to treat me as anything less than an equal. I went into their office and cursed them out from the top down. I was loud, and I was loud on purpose because I wanted every-damn-body to hear me. And then I quit. I left to seek other employment where my abilities and talents were desired and put to good use – by working for myself. I wasn't exactly proud of how loud I got, but I was happy I spoke up and used my voice. I've come too far to not be treated as an equal. Life is too short for that mess.

10

EVOLUTION IS A PROCESS WE CAN'T IGNORE

EVOLUTION:

A process of change by degrees; growth.

We don't change by staying stagnant – by doing the same old thing the same old way day in and day out. Knowing this information is a good thing. It gives you the power to evolve; to move away from whatever you are doing that's wrong and toward doing the things that are right.

The process of evolution isn't easy, nor is it something that happens overnight. Even if you are someone who stopped smoking or drinking cold turkey, you had to evolve from a place of not wanting to smell like smoke or not wake up hung over, in order to get to the place where you said, "No more."

For me, I wanted to be a man that my loved ones could be proud of. When I was a teenager, I remember my *titi*, Margi, asking me if I was going to stop selling drugs. What she was really asking me was if I was going to evolve. If I was going to be the one to change and to break the cycle – or habit – that had been prevalent in my family. At the time, I didn't have an answer for her. It took me a long while to want to really change my hustle, to ignite my drive to learn more, to start something new, to cross t's dot i's. In my twenties and thirties, I sort of thought I had, but I really hadn't.

Here's what I've learned:

1. Nothing is forever. You always have to be evolving as the world evolves. Whatever the current norm is, you should be able to adapt to the change as that norm changes. You have to see it coming.

2. I want my first born and my second born sons to be able to do this. I want them to be able to better prepare themselves for the change that is coming. To not fall behind. To remove fear or anger and just adapt.

3. I did this myself. For work, I found a way to only do what makes me happy and still be just as lucrative. **THAT'S EVOLUTION**. I found a way to be unafraid to take chances, to invest in myself and to not care what others think. **THAT'S EVOLUTION**. Even being able to share these stories so freely with you? **THAT'S EVOLUTION**.

All of these thoughts are an evolution from the man I was. In terms of P.L.U.S.H. and living a life of P.L.U.S.H., here are a few thoughts to remember:

Honesty: There's nothing to lose from being honest. You just have to mentally prepare for the outcome. For example, when I'm struggling, I know that I'll just figure it out. I know this; but I have to be honest about what I'm experiencing. If I'm worried about money, I need to be honest about that and ask for help if I need it. I can't look at asking for help as a flaw. It's ok to ask questions ... Being honest is knowing we don't know everything.

Respect: *I realize that respect is nothing but being polite. It's that simple. If you are a good human, and if you are polite, you will be treated differently – with respect. Just be good to people. Be a good human.*

Wealth: *Family is everything. Back in the day, I felt like I was rich because I had money and status. Now, I have family. I feel richer than ever. (FYI, we're all rich in our own little way. Laughter and love bring wealth too.)*

Power: *Power is knowing that I dictate the penalties and rewards that come from my actions. I am powerful. I am the power because I believe in myself. Outward things are not where the power is.*

Freedom: *I really do believe that freedom is 100% mental. I am free to accept that I have power over my choices. Freedom is doing the right thing. Freedom is the little things, talking to people, hugging your kids, going to the grocery store … the little things.*

As human beings, our evolution process is first mental, then spiritual and then physically. You must evolve mentally before you can evolve spiritually. Before you can evolve physically, you must evolve both mentally and spiritually.

Mentally: You must educate yourself. But, in doing so, you must have the ability to comprehend what you read, see and hear. However, to comprehend, you must have a strong base with which to receive what you are reading, seeing and hearing.

Spiritually: If you are religious, this means you have studied the word of God over and over again, so that you have a strong base within you to keep receiving the word of the Lord.

Physically: If you are a body builder, in order for your muscles to respond to you lifting weights and whatnot, you must start with a strong base, a strong body that is healthy and fortified with protein and carbs to help you see results.

If you are a student (in school, or of the world), you must feed yourself with information, facts or experiences. Those will allow you to comprehend the new information coming to you, so that you eventually become educated. You must comprehend the theory of cause-and-effect, as well as the theory of action-and-reaction.

To evolve, you must be rational. By that I mean level-headed, tolerant, conscious, unprejudiced and unbiased. When you can mentally view life with an open mind and without prejudice or bias, you will be able to truly evolve spiritually. Being spiritual is having a Godly sense of righteousness; it also means being worldly and earthly. In other words, you cannot evolve spiritually if you cause trouble, commit sins, are unruly, shrewd, underhanded, insidious or simply dishonest.

To evolve, you must be honest. With yourself and with others.

CONFESSION

The day the feds came looking for me, I was at work on a forty-foot ladder, painting a house. My friend called me, "Where you at?" I said, "At work, nigga. What?" He said, "The feds just came here looking for you."

That was the first time I was blindsided by law enforcement.

That was the beginning of the end of the beginning. I had just started working, trying to get myself into a place that was out of the streets and legitimately of my own doing. I was in a transitional phase where I had been distancing myself from others, and I was active in my first-born child's life; he was only two years old. I had just picked out a bed for him. I was starting something new for myself.

Because I had been moving around a lot and didn't really have my own address, the feds didn't know where to find me. After my friend called me, though, I had a choice. I could run, or I could turn myself in. I chose to turn myself in. I didn't want the police to be running into my family's homes, looking for me. I didn't want to put any of them in danger or get them caught up in any of my doings, so I did what I felt was the right thing to do.

I went to my girl's place. I smoked, then I got so drunk I could barely see; I had to drink myself into turning myself in or I wouldn't have made it.

I went in after hours because I knew it would be less hectic. I opened the doors of the precinct and walked in.

"Excuse me, we're closed," an officer said.

 84

"You're looking for me. I'm pretty sure they want to see me."

They asked, "Who are you?"

I told them, "I'm from the raid; you all are looking for me."

All hell broke loose. They scattered around, flipping papers and telephones and shit and they took me in. I was so … disappointed.

It wasn't that I thought I was invincible at the time. I just thought I was untouchable. I felt that I was untouchable by the state jurisdiction because I moved good – I was working, living out of state, getting things to where they needed to be. I suppose I felt safe from the feds because I was certainly no Pablo Escobar. I was wrong.

When you get caught, whether it's by the feds, or by your momma for eating candy when she told you not to, you have a choice. You have a choice to change or a choice not to. This process of change is what I call evolution. Now, I've got be honest with you. I didn't start living the P.L.U.S.H. Lyfe the day they got me or even the day I was released. I didn't start living it until I moved into my own apartment several years after I was released. Why? Because even though I started writing the book and developing the principles the very first day I got locked up, I had yet to fully evolve as a person – a person who was ready to change. That part took time, but eventually I got there because I wanted better for myself. I was willing to wait for me (my actions) to catch up to my own principles so that I could live a better life for myself and provide a better life for my family.

I'm so thankful I did.

11

MY FINAL CONFESSION

I hope you enjoyed this book and found it inspirational. Life experiences and an open mind led me to start writing it, but my drive to finish it came from knowing that when I did, it would have a purpose: to help someone.

During my trials and tribulations, I reached deep inside myself to find meaning. In that exploration, I knew I wanted to give to those who felt alone, misunderstood, lost, confused or in doubt about life or the future.

I want you to know that you are successful. You are worthy. You were put on this earth to do something with yourself and for yourself. Don't waste this opportunity on nonsense. I won't say I was given a second chance, but I will say that the powers above wanted me to have another chance at opportunity, at having a successful life.

Success has many definitions. This whole book, in some ways, is about definitions. Ultimately, you get to define how successful you want to be and in what ways.

There are so many ways to better yourself and to become successful. While I was incarcerated, I used to tell everyone that they could better themselves, even while being confined. I knew we had access to resources that many didn't even know about. I used to tell them that there were resources they could use that they wouldn't find in the limited "employment section" of our library. They would have to look in other areas to grow, like psychology, literature, math, economics, business, entertainment or science. It may take some research or a little foot work, but the help and information is there to spark the mind into action. For you, the message is the same. Think about the freedom you have! There are businesses you can start, licenses you can get, investments you can learn about or make. It's all up to you to do some homework instead of being the one pointing the finger at others and making excuses that amount to nothing.

Here are a few inside tips from what I have learned about these untold opportunities (often kept hidden from the public or the unemployed):

1. *Did you know there is an apprenticeship program for many different good paying jobs? All you have to do is go to or contact the Labor (Temple) Union in your city/town. They have an apprenticeship program for painters, electricians, plumbing, masonry, roofing, sheet metal fabrication, etc.*

2. *Did you know you can contact the Department of Tax and Finance and request application(s)to be mailed to you for almost any type of business and/or vendor license? There are so many different licenses to choose from that are all fairly easy to obtain.*

3. *Did you know you really don't need millions to make an investment in the stock market and/or mutual funds? You could also consider investing in CD's and bonds. You could become an investor with as little as $1,000. A little research on the market is all it takes. You can go online to Investopedia.com for help or buy the book Secrets for Profiting in Bull and Bear Markets. (This book was published in 1988 but offers good information.) There are a number of books on learning how to become an investor. Explore!*

4. *Did you know that you can start a website for free? There are many platforms to use that have free subscription tiers to get you started. Check out wordpress.com, squarspace.com or wix.com.*

5. *Did you know that you can find help with almost any service like graphic design, virtual assistants, copywriting, newsletter writing, or photography*

for a little as $5.00? Go to fiverr.com to learn more. (If you are good at something or have a skill that someone else may need, you can also set up your own account and make some passive income.)

6. *Did you know that you can do anything you set your mind to doing?*

Whatever it is you want to become or accomplish in life, it's possible. With a little research and determination anything is possible. Always remember closed minds and closed mouths don't get fed, so don't be afraid to ask questions or use any means to gain all of the information available. One thing I realized is that information and opportunities are right in front of our faces. Don't be deaf, dumb or blind to life's opportunities.

Also, to capitalize on the opportunity that is coming, here are **7 Tools Needed for Success**:

- Good manners and hygiene (maintain a presentable appearance).
- Good reading, writing and comprehension skills.
- Good listening skills, people skills and communication skills.
- Willingness to learn and accept constructive criticism.
- Confidence, motivation and ambition.
- Mental and physical strength to handle responsibility.
- Respect, loyalty and honesty.

If I were a preacher, I'd be preaching the gospel of opportunity. Today, I am all about looking for land to purchase so that my family and I can start to build generational wealth for our kids and those who come after us. I am a licensed in painter; I can work directly with companies, or I can freelance. I am never without an opportunity to make income. I also own trademarks and business in multiple areas; I diversify opportunities to enjoy life and take care of my family. You can do the same thing. While you create opportunities, just know that you can't do everything at once. Choose one thing that you want to accomplish, go after it and then go onto the next.

I'll leave you with this. It is a quote I found a long time ago and it still means something to me today. Cecil B. DeMille, the film director and producer said, "It is impossible for us to break the law. We can only break ourselves against the law."

SPECIAL THANKS

This is the life I lived; it's what I've learned. Going into federal prison was my rock bottom and it made me look at myself. It made me think about what type of man I wanted my first-born son to know me as. I say my first-born because he was there when this all happened. He was on my mind; he was my life. I had just dropped off my son and went in to work the day the feds found me. I was always thinking of him.

Whatever people would have said about me in the streets was one thing, but I knew I had power over my own words. I had the ability to tell him, personally, what I believed he needed to be aware of and what he should be mindful of as he grew into a man – without me.

I paid a lot of prices; being like me was not going to get him to where I wanted him to be. That's not to say I'm not a bad person. There's nothing wrong with me. I just didn't want him to be me. I wanted a new life for him.

So, to my son, I say thank you for things you'll never understand.

Family is everything to me. There were so many families (by blood and otherwise) that played a major role in me becoming the man I am today, yet these family members had the biggest impact: Tonia Otero, Deborah Hunter, Mariana Gonzalez, Delia Rosario, George Roman, Darell W. Perry, Kim Riley, Jessica Hinds, Jaime Gonzalez, Luis E. Gonzalez, Luis A. Gonzalez, My Gonzalez/Roman/Rosario/Newton Family, Tito Velez & Family. Additionally, Robert Crutch & Family, Sabrina, Carla, Nina & my Davis Family, my Jordan Family, my Soto Family, my Davila Family, Jessica Colon & my Colon/Soto Family, Erika Melanie & my Riddick Family, Anne-Marie, Victoria Gorman, my New Lots Family and my Cozine Family.

I also want to thank and pay respect to those who have passed on and really meant something to me. I am a product of all of them in some way because they were a part of the village that raised me and warmly welcomed me into their world. For them, I have nothing but love. So, in loving memory: Petronila O. Santana, Pedro L. Gonzalez, John H. Newton, Jose Otero, Angel Martinez, Jose Andujar, Ruben Roman, Jermell Hayes, Nadine Caban, Maria Soto, Ana Reyes, Elizabeth Davila and Victoria Wise. (This is as far as I will go because, unfortunately, there have been too many losses throughout my life. #GoneYetNeverForgotten)

Finally, I thank those who physically helped make this book happen. I would like to send the biggest thanks to my Real Wize Family. First, to the man known as my uncle, my brother and my friend Wilfredo (Wize El Jefe) Otero for giving me the motivation I needed and for believing in me when nobody else did. Hasta La Muerte my brother! Second, a big, big thanks to Brandy (Ms. Joy) for believing in us enough to share her crafts in creating the Real Wize brand.

This book would still be a draft if it hadn't been for Parul Agrawal whose gracious desire to help me publish led me to my editor and wordsmith, Peppur Chambers. To Peppur, I say, wow! I can't begin to thank you enough for taking the gig, for seeing more to the book than what I had presented, and for believing in me and all that I aim to achieve. Thank you for being a visionary and giving this book what it needed most, the touch of a woman.

Lastly, I thank my second-born son, Jaelin Jermell Gonzalez, a.k.a. The Prince, who often had to wait longer than he wanted for popsicles or a bedtime story while his papi was working on making his own dreams come true.

ABOUT THE AUTHOR

Anthony J. Gonzalez is self-defined as a simple man. He is a father, a brother, and an uncle. He is a Leo, and rightfully so; a king from the county of Kings, New York.

His goal is to be a better man, in whatever forms of life that may mean. He strives to constantly learn. With this, he is at peace.

Anthony believes prevention is better than the cure and hopes that incorporating this theory outside of prison will inspire others to incorporate it in their lives.

This book is evidence of all that he is, hopes to be, and hopes for his readers to become.

Contact information:
This book is presented by myself and Real Wize Productions.
Email: realwizeproductions@gmail.com
Website: realwizeproductions.com
IG: @real_wize718
IG: @papi_jae73

Made in the USA
Middletown, DE
20 November 2024

64973458R00059